Nasty Names Are I

An Australian white ibis responds to name-calling in the city

Written & Illustrated

by

Rick LeCouteur

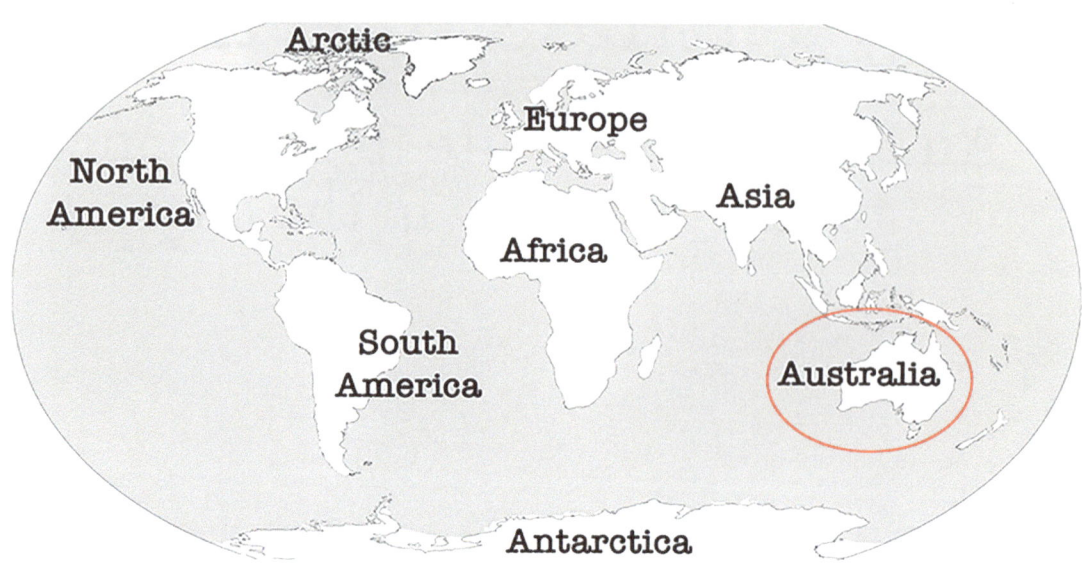

Nasty Names Are Hurtful
© 2024 by Rick LeCouteur
All rights reserved.
ISBN: 979-8-218-46111-9

Australian white ibis (*Threskiornis molucca*)

Thoth

Thoth was an ancient Egyptian deity depicted in hieroglyphs as a man with the head of an ibis.

Thoth was the god of the moon, wisdom, knowledge, writing, science, magic, art, and judgment.

"You're a dirty bin chicken!" squawked the Australian raven from its perch on a streetlight. "You lurk near restaurants, eating scraps! You don't belong here!"

Penny was confused. She knew that the raven wasn't supposed to be in the city either.

[*A "trash can" in America is called a "bin" or "rubbish bin" in Australia*]

Penny, an Australian white ibis, turned her head, trying to ignore the unkind words.

But the hurtful names made her sad ...

"Sandwich snatcher!" jeered the rock dove. "You're a scavenger stealing food from unsuspecting people."

Penny remained silent, but the words hurt deeply ...

She knew that pigeons were the most aggressive scavengers in the city.

Many other birds called Penny hurtful names.

"Dumpster diver!" yelled the Australian magpie.

Penny walked away ...

She had often seen magpies stealing food scraps from rubbish bins.

"Picnic pirate!" shouted the masked lapwing.

Penny chose not to respond …

She had seen the lapwings lingering around picnics waiting for handouts.

"Flying rat!" called out the silver gull.

This was hurtful, as Penny had seen many silver gulls scavenging for food scraps in the city.

She didn't utter a word ...

"Tip turkey!" cried the Australian sulfur-crested cockatoo from its nest in a hollow tree.

Penny, the Australian white ibis, remained silent ...

[*A "landfill" in America is referred to as a "tip" in Australia*]

"What do those names mean?" Penny wondered. "They really hurt my feelings."

"I'll ask my mom what to do. She always knows how to handle tough situations."

That night, as she was about to fall asleep in a palm tree, Penny asked her mom about the name-calling.

Penny's mom replied "Be proud to be an Australian white ibis. Our ancestors were admired in ancient Egypt as symbols of Thoth, the god who maintained the universe. People were happy to let us walk beside them through the city streets."

Penny's Mom continued "Ibis lived in Australia long before the first humans arrived on the continent. When the aboriginal people settled in Australia thousands of years ago, we lived together peacefully. Life was good. The aboriginal people took care of us and our wetland homes."

"Then, as more people settled in Australia, our family moved to the city because our wetland homes were destroyed by humans and droughts. Our natural environment was lost. We had no food and were hungry. What else could we do but find a new place to live?"

"At first, we moved to the city parks and lived in the palm trees, which reminded us of the wetland grasses we had left behind."

"Then, while searching for food in the parks, we noticed people tossing half-eaten food and trash onto the streets."

"So, we learned to hide, watch, and wait for people to toss their trash or leave uneaten food on plates at lunch tables."

"We did this only to survive."

"Most of us only ate food that people had abandoned or thrown away."

"Over time, we learned we could survive on the food scraps that fell onto the streets and the bin-juice that dripped from the rubbish bins."

[Bin-juice is the smelly liquid that accumulates at the bottom of a garbage can]

"A few of us resorted to eating food scraps from inside the rubbish bins," said Penny's mom.

"We only did this because the garbage bins were overflowing and lacked lids."

"Sometimes people in the parks would talk to us and offer food," Penny's mom said.

"Other times they would chase us away from their picnics. It was very confusing to be an Australian white ibis in the city."

"Then people started to call us nasty names like bin chicken, tip turkey and picnic pirate."

"Over time, people began blaming us for the rubbish on the streets, even though it was the people themselves leaving the mess," Penny's mom explained.

"We didn't choose to live in the city. We're environmental refugees, forced out of our natural home by humans."

"Be proud that the Australian white ibis has found a way to coexist with people in the city," Penny's mom said.

"We are beautiful Australian birds, playing a crucial role in controlling insect populations and maintaining the health of wetlands. In rural areas we are known as the farmer's friend because our long beaks help break apart the soil."

"Despite our gentle nature, and preference to live far from the city, we are left with no choice but to survive wherever we can."

Penny's mom finished by saying "Remember, the Australian white ibis is native to Australia and lived here long before people arrived."

"Penny, you did the right thing by ignoring the nasty names and walking away. You also did the right thing by sharing your feelings with me."

"I am so proud to be your mom."

Penny felt happy thinking about her mom's words. As she settled down to sleep, she imagined what she would say if humans could understand her.

She would say "Instead of calling us nasty names and chasing us away, why not focus on positive actions? Restore the wetlands and help us return to our natural habitat. Dispose of your rubbish properly, close the rubbish bin lids, and keep the streets clean."

Australian white ibis are beautiful, amazing, and resilient birds," thought Penny as she fell asleep.

The next day when Penny woke up, her dad was beside her. The words he said would stay with her forever.

"Penny, you are a beautiful bird. Your elegant feathers shimmer with every movement. Your long, curved beak is perfect for finding delicious snacks in the mud. You have a graceful neck that can stretch out for food or tuck under a wing for sleep, and your beautiful wing feathers will carry you high in the sky. Your stunning eyes reflect curiosity and intelligence."

"I am so proud to be your dad."

There is a quiet dignity, and a touch of mystery surrounding the Australian white ibis. So, next time you see one, take a moment to appreciate its beauty. Don't chase it and don't call it nasty names.

Admire each movement, every feather, and every feature, and appreciate the story of a remarkable and enchanting creature in the world of birds.

Information for parents and teachers

The Australian white ibis, a native wetland bird, has been forced into urban areas due to habitat degradation. Historically, it thrived in inland wetlands, alongside other species of ibis, such as the sacred ibis of ancient Egypt. However, changes in land use and water management led to habitat deterioration and depleted food sources.

As a result, many ibis migrated to urban centers, adapting to scavenging from landfill sites and rubbish bins. In cities, their presence can be disruptive due to noise and odor, earning them derogatory nicknames like sandwich snatcher and bin chicken.

Despite this negative perception, ibises play a crucial role in urban ecosystems by aerating soil and controlling insect populations. With proper management, urban environments can become mutually beneficial for both ibises and humans, offering educational opportunities and fostering a greater appreciation for nature.

What can people do for the ibis?

- Encourage respectful behavior towards ibises, emphasizing the importance of not harming or harassing them.

- Discourage feeding ibises or leaving food scraps or trash around.

- Ensure that all garbage lids are securely closed.

- Advocate for waste reduction and the removal of potential ibis' attractions, such as water sources and pet food in outdoor areas.

- Suggest avoiding the planting of trees favored by ibises for roosting, such as exotic palms.

- Appreciate the captivating beauty and adaptability of the Australian white ibis by discussing its urban presence and the reasons behind it.

Milton Keynes UK
Ingram Content Group UK Ltd.
UKHW051505221024
2315UKWH00001B/1